Breaking the Shackles:

A Personal Journey to Freedom from Porn Addiction

Erik L. Current

Table Of Contents

CHAPTER ONE: INTRODUCTION

The prevalence and controversy surrounding pornography have grown in the modern world. While it may offer a momentary escape or release, it can also turn into a destructive and addictive force in people's lives. You may not be well aware of the damaging effects that a porn addiction can have on your relationships, career, and general well-being. But there is still hope.

We will examine the underlying factors that contribute to porn addiction in this book and offer helpful tips and encouragement for overcoming it. You'll discover how to escape the cycle of addiction and achieve lasting freedom and fulfillment. We will also talk about the frequently ignored emotional and interpersonal aspects of recovery and provide resources for ongoing help.

We aim to offer a thorough and sympathetic manual for anyone attempting to beat a porn addiction through a combination of professional insights and personal experiences. This book is for you if you're prepared to take charge of your life and begin the road to recovery. Sit tight and buckle up.

WHAT IS PORNOGRAPHY?

Pornography is the representation of sexual behavior in literature, periodicals, photographs, movies, or other forms of media with the intention of provoking the viewer. It can be presented in a variety of ways, including the written word, pictures, videos, and interactive media. Although pornography has a long history that dates back to ancient civilizations, the proliferation of the internet has made it a more contentious and pervasive problem in modern times.

Pornography can be divided into different categories depending on the medium used, the subjects depicted, and the target audience. It may take the form of more subdued sexual stimulation or explicit depictions of sexual activity. Pornography can also be divided into "softcore," which tends to be less explicit and may not show penetration or genitalia, and "hardcore," which is more explicit and may show a variety of sexual activities and fetishes.

Due to its potential to have detrimental effects on both individuals and society, pornography has frequently been the focus of discussion and criticism. Some contend that it objectifies and degrades women, reinforces harmful gender roles and stereotypes, and can lead to unhealthy attitudes toward sex and relationships. Others contend that when used responsibly, it can be a form of free expression and can improve interpersonal relationships.

RECENT DATA ON PORNOGRAPHY AND IT'S USAGE

There is a sizable presence of pornography on the internet, which is a multi-billion dollar industry. Due to the industry's underground and frequently illegal nature, as well as the internet's and technology's ever-evolving state, it is challenging to determine the size and scope of the sector with accuracy. Insight into the prevalence, consumption trends, and potential effects of pornography can be gained from research and data on the subject.

Because of the widespread use of the internet and mobile devices, there is now a significantly greater availability and accessibility of pornography. The Pornhub Insights blog reports that the website received over 42 billion visits in 2019, with the United States, India, and China ranking as the top three countries in terms of traffic. The data also showed that the average visit lasted around 10 minutes, and that the most common search terms were "lesbian," "teen," and "step mom.". ".

Research has also shown that different genders have different patterns of pornography consumption, with men typically being more likely than women to do so. 43 percent of women and 73 percent of men, according to a study in the Journal of Sex Research, admitted to watching porn in the previous year. The research also showed that men who watched more pornographic content reported feeling more sexually satisfied than they did about their romantic relationships.

While some contend that, when viewed responsibly, pornography can have positive effects on people's lives and relationships, others contend that it can reinforce negative stereotypes and gender roles, objectify women, and encourage harmful attitudes and behaviors toward them. More research is required to fully understand the potential effects of pornography on people and society because they are complicated and contentious.

TYPES OF PORNOGRAPHY

Based on the media used, the subjects depicted, and the intended audience, there are many different types of pornography that can be categorized in different ways. Here are some illustrations:

- Erotic literature that depicts sexual fantasies or behaviors is referred to as written pornography. Examples include novels, short stories, and poems.

- Visual pornography is the term for images, movies, and videos that show nakedness or suggestive sexual behavior. It can range from "softcore" images that are less explicit and might not show genitalia or penetration to "hardcore" images that are more explicit and might show a variety of sexual activities and fetishes.

- Websites, video games, and other online media that let users interact with sexual content or partake in virtual sexual activity are referred to as interactive pornography.

- Pornography that appeals to particular interests or fetishes, such as BDSM, foot fetishism, or voyeurism, is referred to as niche pornography.

- Amateur pornography is defined as homemade material that is frequently created and shared online.

- Pornography that is produced and distributed by well-known companies and is widely accessible is referred to as mainstream pornography.

- Pornography that features males engaging in sexual activity is referred to as gay pornography.

- Pornography that features women having sex with other women is referred to as lesbian pornography.

- Pornography that features transgender or non-binary people is referred to as trans-sexual pornography.

- Explicit images or videos of celebrities are included in celebrity pornography.

- Pornography that shows intimate relationships between family members or close relatives is referred to as incest pornography.

- Pornography that shows minors or kids under the age of 18 having sex or being portrayed in a sexual way is referred to as "child pornography.". It is prohibited in most nations and is frequently connected to child sex abuse.

- Pornography used as a means of vengeance or harassment includes sexually explicit pictures or videos that are shared without the subject's knowledge.

It's important to emphasize once more that these divisions are not all-inclusive and that there is frequently overlap between them. Furthermore, it's critical to understand that pornography is a contentious and complex topic, and that these categories don't necessarily represent everyone's opinions or beliefs.

PORNOGRAPHY ADDICTION

The behavioral addiction known as pornography addiction, also known as compulsive pornography use or hypersexual disorder, is characterized by a persistent and escalating pattern of pornography consumption that interferes with a person's day-to-day activities, interpersonal relationships, and general well-being. The Diagnostic and Statistical Manual of Mental Disorders (DSM-5) of the American Psychiatric Association does not currently recognize it as a diagnosable disorder, but the

International Classification of Diseases (ICD-11) of the World Health Organization does.

Pornography addiction is thought to share similarities with other behavioral addictions, like gambling and gaming, as well as drug addictions. Genetics, early experiences, and environmental influences are just a few of the biological, psychological, and social factors that are thought to play a role in it. Addiction to pornography has been linked to other mental health issues, including personality disorders, depression, and anxiety.

SIGNS AND SYMPTOMS OF PORNOGRAPHY ADDICTION

Here are some warning signs and symptoms to watch out for if you or someone you know may be suffering from a pornography addiction:

- An inability to restrain or cut back on the consumption of pornography, can include their inability to stop using it, stop thinking about it, or reduce the amount of time they spend doing so.

- A preoccupation with pornography that results in distress or anxiety is referred to as an obsession with pornography. This can involve obsessively focusing on pornography to the point where it interferes with other activities and interests.

- Pornography addiction can be reflected as neglecting obligations or relationships, financial difficulties, or issues with one's physical or mental health.

- When unable to access or use pornography, withdrawal symptoms may include agitation, anxiety, or depression.

- Using porn as a coping strategy could involve using the medium to deal with stress, unpleasant feelings, or other issues in life.

It's important to note that these symptoms can differ from person to person and don't always indicate that someone is having problems with a pornography addiction. It is important to seek professional assistance if you are worried about someone else's or your own use of pornography.

IMPACTS OF A PORNOGRAPHY ADDICTION ON A PERSON.

Pornography addiction has a wide range of effects on people and may have an impact on many different areas of their lives. The following categories can aid in understanding how a person's pornography addiction affects them:

PHYSICAL IMPACT

The possible physical effects of a pornography addiction on a person are outlined below in detail:.

- Sleep disorders: Pornography addiction can cause sleep issues, such as trouble falling or staying asleep or poorer-quality sleep.

- Sexual dysfunction: Problems with orgasm, difficulty getting or staying sexy, and other sexual dysfunctions may be linked to addiction to pornography.

- Internet-related injuries: Because of the excessive use of the internet, a pornography addiction can result in physical ailments like carpal tunnel syndrome or back issues.

- Changes in Brain Function and Structure: Addiction to pornography may be accompanied by changes in brain regions that are involved in motivation, judgment, and impulse control. These changes may make it more difficult to resist the urge to use pornography and may help compulsive behavior to emerge.

- Changes in Brain Chemistry: Dopamine and serotonin levels may be out of balance in people who become addicted to pornography, which can have an impact on a person's motivation, pleasure perception, and mood.

- Immune system weakened: Chronic stress, which is connected to porn addiction, has been linked to a weakened immune system, which can make someone more susceptible to illness.

- Cardiovascular issues: The risk of cardiovascular issues, such as heart disease, may increase as a result of chronic stress and other detrimental effects on mental health that are connected to pornography addiction.

- Reduced exercise: Addiction to pornography may result in a less active lifestyle and reduced exercise, which can increase the risk of developing chronic diseases and other health issues like obesity.

It's crucial to keep in mind that the physical effects of a pornography addiction can differ from person to person and depend on a number of variables, including the severity of the addiction and other health conditions. Furthermore, there is a dearth of research on the physical effects of pornography addiction, and more study is required to fully comprehend the problem.

SPIRITUAL IMPACT

It is crucial to remember that the idea of spirituality is highly individual and subjective, and that each person will define spiritual impact differently. Here are a few ways that a person's addiction to pornography might have an effect on their spirituality:

- Pornography addiction can result in distorted beliefs and values about sex, relationships, and oneself, which may be in opposition to a person's personal spiritual beliefs and values.

- Feelings of Guilt and Shame: Pornography addiction can result in feelings of guilt and shame, which can have an impact on a person's sense of self-worth and connection to a higher power or spirituality.

- Loss of Connection With Others: Porn addiction can strain or harm relationships, leading to a feeling of isolation and a loss of connection with others. This can have an impact on a person's sense of belonging and community.

- Loss Of Purpose: A pornographic addiction may take up all of a person's time and energy, blurring their focus on other aspects of life and leaving them feeling aimless.

The impact of pornography addiction on a person's spirituality can take many different forms and can differ greatly from person to person. It's important to remember this. Seeking assistance from a qualified professional or a spiritual advisor may be beneficial if you are worried about how your pornography addiction is affecting your spiritual health.

SOCIAL IMPACT

An individual's social life may be negatively impacted by a porn addiction in a number of ways. Porn addiction may have the following negative effects on relationships and social interactions:

- Intimate relationship issues: Porn addiction can cause issues with intimacy, communication, and trust in relationships. It might also result in a lack of interest in in-person sex or a preference for porn over in-person intimacy.

- Isolation and social withdrawal: People who are addicted to porn may spend a lot of time watching porn, which can cause social isolation and a withdrawal from social activities.

- Communication and social interaction issues: Porn addiction can make it difficult for a person to communicate and interact with others on a meaningful level.

- Setting and upholding healthy boundaries in relationships can be difficult for someone who is addicted to porn because they may struggle to distinguish between appropriate and inappropriate behavior.

- Relationship tension: A person who is addicted to porn may prioritize their addiction over their obligations and commitments to others, which can strain relationships with friends and family.

- Shame and stigma: Many people who battle a porn addiction might experience shame or stigma about their actions, which can result in social isolation and a reluctance to ask for help or support from others.

- Employment challenges: Porn addiction may cause issues with attendance and productivity at work, which can harm a person's chances of finding a job and advancing in their career.

- Reputational harm: People who are addicted to porn may suffer reputational damage because they may be thought to be irresponsible or unrespectful of others. An individual's interpersonal relationships, both at work and at home, may suffer as a result.

In general, a person's relationships and social life can suffer from a number of negative effects from a porn addiction. It's critical for people with porn addiction to get help in order to address these problems and learn constructive coping mechanisms.

PROFESSIONAL IMPACT

A person's professional life may suffer from a variety of consequences due to their porn addiction. On the job and in the workplace, porn addiction could have the following effects:

- Concentration and productivity issues: Because a porn addict may be preoccupied with thoughts of porn or may watch a lot of porn during work hours, this can make it difficult for them to concentrate and be productive at their jobs.

- Attendance problems: People who are addicted to porn may have trouble keeping up with their obligations and commitments at work, including issues with attendance, punctuality, and completing tasks on schedule.

- Colleague issues: As the person may struggle with boundaries, respect, and appropriate behavior in the workplace, porn addiction may cause issues with communication and interpersonal relationships.

- Legal problems: Some people who are addicted to porn may partake in unlawful activities, such as downloading or disseminating child pornography, which can harm a person's career prospects and cause legal issues.

- Porn addiction can cause issues with attendance, productivity, and job performance, which can put a person at risk of losing their job.

- Making decisions is difficult, and this can make it difficult for someone to do their job well. Porn addiction may cause decision-making and judgment issues.

- Reduced job satisfaction: Being addicted to porn can make someone unhappy at work or feel as though their addiction makes it difficult for them to do their job well.

- Obstacles to career advancement: Porn addiction may result in issues with one's reputation and relationships with subordinates and superiors, which may limit one's chances for career advancement.

IMPACT OF PORNOGRAPHY ADDICTION ON A FAMILY

A person's family life may be negatively impacted by a porn addiction in a number of ways. The following are some possible consequences of porn addiction on family relationships:

- Relationship strain: A person who is addicted to porn may prioritize their addiction over their obligations and commitments to their family, which can strain relationships with spouses, partners, and kids.

- Problems with communication and trust in family relationships can result from a person's addiction to pornography because they may find it difficult to be open and honest about their behavior.

- Conflict and tension: Porn addiction can cause conflict and tension in the family because other family members might be worried about the addict's behavior or might feel hurt or betrayed by their addiction.

- Emotional distance: Because of their addiction or feelings of guilt or shame, people who are addicted to pornography may grow emotionally distant from their family members.

- Neglect of obligations: Because of the potential for prioritizing one's addiction over their obligations to their family, porn addiction may result in the neglect of obligations and commitments to the family.

- Financial difficulties: Porn addiction can cause financial difficulties because the addict may spend a lot of money on porn or may neglect their family's financial needs.

- Reduced intimacy and sexual dysfunction: Porn addiction may cause reduced intimacy and sexual dysfunction in relationships with a spouse or partner, which may be detrimental to the family's general health and happiness.

- Parenting may suffer as a result of a person's addiction to pornography because they may be preoccupied with it or find it difficult to set up boundaries and give their kids the right kind of guidance.

Overall, a porn addict's family life and relationships may suffer as a result of their addiction. In order to address these issues and learn healthy coping mechanisms, it is crucial for people who are suffering from a porn addiction to get help.

IMPACTS OF PORN ADDICTION ON SOCIETY

Numerous harmful effects on society may result from porn addiction. There may be a variety of social consequences of porn addiction.

- Reduced output: Porn addiction can cause issues with output and attendance at work, which can have a negative impact on a person's employment and career prospects as well as wider economic ramifications.

- Legal issues: Some porn addicts may engage in illegal activities, such as downloading or disseminating child pornography, which can have negative social and legal repercussions.

- Health issues: Porn addiction can result in a variety of physical and mental health issues, which can have social and economic repercussions.

- Impact on kids and teens: Teens who are exposed to porn may develop distorted ideas about relationships and sexuality, which may have long-term effects on their ability to cope socially and emotionally.

- Person exploitation and objectification: Pornography may help to exploit and objectify people, especially women and other marginalized groups.

- Promotion of unwholesome attitudes and actions: Pornography may encourage unwholesome attitudes and actions, such as coercion and violence, which can have detrimental effects on society.

- Sexual assault and harassment, for example, could become more commonplace as a result of the widespread availability of pornography.

- Contribution to gender inequality: By supporting negative stereotypes and the objectification and denigration of women, pornography may contribute to gender inequality.

Overall, porn addiction can have detrimental effects on society, including adverse effects on children and young people, objectification and exploitation of people, promotion of unhealthy attitudes and behaviors, normalization of harmful behaviors, and contribution to gender inequality.

CHAPTER TWO: UNDERSTANDING THE FACTORS THAT LEAD TO PORN ADDICTION

Porn addiction can have several different causes. Instead, the emergence of a pornographic addiction is frequently the result of a number of factors working together. The following are some possible causes of porn addiction.

PSYCHOLOGICAL AND EMOTIONAL FACTORS

The emergence of a pornographic addiction may be influenced by a variety of psychological and emotional factors. A few possible psychological and emotional triggers for a porn addiction include:.

- Low self-esteem: As a coping mechanism for self-deprecating feelings, those who have low self-esteem may be more susceptible to developing a porn addiction.

- Porn can be a temporary escape from stress and anxiety for people who are experiencing these conditions.

- Porn can be a self-medication strategy for depression or a way to numb unpleasant emotions.

- Loneliness: Some individuals may use porn to help them deal with feelings of isolation or loneliness.

- Boredom: Using porn as a way to kill time or get rid of boredom is possible.

- Problems with real-life intimacy: Some individuals may use porn as a coping mechanism for issues or difficulties with real-life intimacy and relationships.

It is important to know and note these factors as they are vital in kicking porn addiction.

SOCIAL AND CULTURAL FACTORS

The emergence of a pornographic addiction may be influenced by a variety of social and cultural factors. The following are some possible social and cultural elements that may support a porn addiction.

- Early pornographic exposure: Early exposure to pornography may increase the risk of later-life addiction development.

- Pornography acceptance in society: Residing in a society where pornography acceptance is higher may increase the risk of addiction.

- Peer pressure: Having friends or peers expose you to pornography may make you more likely to become addicted.

- Limited access to healthy coping strategies: People who lack access to supportive networks or healthy coping strategies may be more likely to use pornography as a coping mechanism for stressful or negative feelings.

- Traditional gender roles and expectations may contribute to the development of a porn addiction because some people may feel under pressure to conform to particular sexual expectations or may feel ashamed of their sexual desires.

BIOLOGICAL AND BRAIN CHEMISTRY FACTORS

It is possible that certain brain chemicals and biological elements contribute to the emergence of a pornographic addiction, according to the available evidence. These are a few biological and brain chemistry variables that could be involved in the development of a porn addiction.

- The brain chemical dopamine plays a role in pleasure and reward. It's possible for someone to develop an addiction to the pleasure and reward they get from dopamine-releasing activities like watching pornography.

- Genetics: According to research, genetics may be involved in how addiction develops. An addiction to pornography may be more likely to develop in people with a family history of addiction.

- Hormonal imbalances: Hormonal imbalances, such as low testosterone levels, may make it more likely for someone to become addicted to porn.

- Repeated exposure to pornography has been linked to altered brain chemistry, which, according to research, may play a role in the emergence of an addiction.

- The brain has a system of reward pathways, which are opened up when a person partakes in pleasurable activities. These pathways are activated when someone watches pornography, which may aid in the emergence of an addiction.

- Tolerance: Just like with other addictions, repeated exposure to pornography can result in tolerance, which means that the person needs to view increasingly extreme or intense pornography in order to experience the same level of pleasure.

- Withdrawal: When a person tries to stop watching pornography, they might encounter withdrawal symptoms like irritability, anxiety, or cravings. It might be challenging for the person to stop viewing pornography as a result of these symptoms.

- Disorders that can co-occur with porn addiction include anxiety, depression, and substance abuse. This can make treatment and recovery more difficult.

- The brain is capable of adapting and changing, a process known as neuroplasticity, according to research. The brain's structure and functioning may change as a result of behaviors like watching pornography, which may aid in the emergence of addictions.

This chapter has exposed the factors that can contribute to the formation of a Pornography addiction by categorizing then into Psychological, Biological and Social factors. A crucial step of solving a problem is understanding why the problem exists, that is the aim of this chapter, to better understand pornography addiction.

CHAPTER THREE: ADDRESSING THE UNDERLYING ISSUES

We have seen some causes of pornography addiction, next we will examine some of these causes and highlight ways to deal with them.

STRESS

Stress is a normal part of everyday life and can come from a variety of sources, such as work, relationships, financial problems, and health concerns. While a small amount of stress can be beneficial as it can help people perform under pressure and motivate them to meet deadlines, excessive stress can have negative effects on both physical and mental health.

Here are a few strategies that may be helpful in managing stress and overcoming a pornography addiction:

- Exercise: Exercising regularly can improve your mood and reduce stress.

Try going for a walk, jog, or bike ride; joining a gym; or signing up for a class.

- Improve your focus and reduce your stress by practicing mindfulness. You can practice mindfulness by engaging in activities like yoga, deep breathing, and meditation.

- Find social support: Having relationships with friends and family can make you feel like you belong and can be a great source of solace when you're stressed.

- Take breaks: By taking regular breaks from your work and other obligations, you'll have more time to relax and reenergize.

- Get enough sleep: Sleep is crucial for reducing stress and maintaining overall health. Every night, get between seven and nine hours of sleep.

- Seek expert advice: If you're having trouble controlling your stress on your own, you might want to consider seeking advice from a mental health professional.

Therapy can help people identify and treat their stress's underlying causes as well as develop useful coping skills.

Remember that each person is different, so what works for one person might not work for someone else. It might be useful to try out a few different strategies in order to find the stress-reduction techniques that are most effective for you.

BOREDOM

Boredom is a feeling of disinterest or lack of excitement. It is a common feeling that most people experience at some point in their lives. Boredom can be caused by a lack of stimulation, a lack of goals or purpose, or a lack of challenges.

Boredom may be a common trigger for those who battle a porn addiction because it can provide a brief release from boredom or restlessness. Some strategies to beat boredom and lessen your propensity to turn to pornography are as follows:.

- Find a pastime or activity you enjoy: Engaging in pursuits that make you feel good and provide a sense of accomplishment can help you feel less bored and provide a useful outlet for your energy.

- Make more friends: Making new friends is a great way to combat boredom. Consider inviting friends or family over for a get-together, joining a club, or joining a group if you want to meet new people.

- Become involved in your community: Volunteering or performing community service can be a rewarding way to spend your time.

- Take breaks and give yourself time to unwind: Boredom can occasionally be a sign of overwork or burnout, so it's important to give yourself time to rest and relax.

- Seek professional help: You may want to consider seeking help from a mental health professional if you find that your porn addiction is making it difficult for you to deal with boredom or other issues.

Explore the causes of your addiction in therapy while developing healthy coping skills.

LONELINESS

Loneliness is a feeling of isolation or disconnection from others. It is a common emotion that most people experience at some point in their lives, but for some people it can become chronic and have negative effects on their overall well-being.

Loneliness can be a frequent trigger for those who struggle with a porn addiction because pornography can momentarily provide an escape from feelings of isolation. Here are some methods that might help you deal with your loneliness while lowering your risk of turning to pornography:.

- Connect with others: Engaging in social activity can help you fight loneliness. If you want to meet new people, think about joining a club or family group, inviting friends or family over, or hosting a party.

- A rewarding way to pass the time and make a difference in the lives of others is through volunteer work or community service.

- Self-care is crucial because taking care of your emotional and physical needs can make you feel happier overall and less lonely.

- Seek professional help if necessary: If you're having trouble controlling your loneliness or other issues brought on by your porn addiction, you might want to consider seeking out a mental health professional's assistance. Create sound coping strategies and investigate the causes of your addiction in therapy.

- Consider getting a pet: Owning a pet not only provides companionship but can also be a great source of support and comfort.

ANGER

Anger is a normal emotion that everyone experiences from time to time. It is a natural reaction to situations that we find frustrating, annoying or unfair.

Despite being a common and normal emotion, anger can be challenging to manage and control. Here are some techniques to control your rage and reduce the likelihood that you will turn to pornography:

- Analyze what is causing you to be angry in order to identify the source of your rage. You can manage your anger more skillfully if you recognize where it comes from.

- To help you feel calmer, practice relaxation techniques. There are several efficient techniques, including deep breathing, progressive muscle relaxation, and mindfulness meditation.

- Seek social support: Talking about your anger with a friend, member of your family, or a therapist can help you process and deal with your emotions.

- Exercise: Exercising can be a helpful way to let go of pent-up tension and lessen angry feelings.

- Seek professional help: You might want to consider seeking assistance from a mental health professional if you find that you are having trouble controlling your anger or other issues related to your porn addiction. As well as helping you develop healthy coping mechanisms, therapy can be a helpful way to look into and address the underlying causes of your addiction.

It's important to remember that recovering from a porn addiction requires effort and patience, and that finding healthy coping mechanisms may take some time. Always remember to be kind to yourself and ask for help when you need it.

DEPRESSION

Depression is a mental disorder characterized by persistent feelings of sadness, hopelessness, and a lack of interest or pleasure in activities. It can also cause a variety of physical and emotional symptoms, such as changes in appetite and sleep patterns, difficulty concentrating, and decreased energy.

Addiction to pornography can both cause and contribute to depressive symptoms. As a result, treating and managing depression can be a crucial component of quitting a pornographic addiction.

Here are a few methods for battling depression and kicking a pornography habit.

- Seek assistance: If you're struggling with depression and pornographic addiction, it may be helpful to speak with a therapist or join a support group. Support from others can help you feel connected and understood while also assisting you in creating effective coping mechanisms.

- Take part in enjoyable activities: Having fun and feeling accomplished when you do things you enjoy can make you feel better and less inclined to watch porn.

- Self-care is crucial for managing depression. This includes both physical and emotional wellbeing. Indulging in relaxation exercises like deep breathing or meditation can be part of this, along with getting enough sleep, eating a healthy diet, and other lifestyle choices.

- Seek treatment: If your depression is severe or interfering with your daily life, it may be necessary for you to get help from a mental health professional. Treatment for depression typically entails a combination of therapy and medication, and it can be a useful way to manage symptoms and enhance general wellbeing.

- Be patient and kind to yourself as you go through the process. It takes time and effort to overcome an addiction and manage depression. Consider consulting a mental health professional or joining a support group if you feel you need more assistance.

PEER PRESSURE

When attempting to kick a porn habit, peer pressure can be a difficult obstacle to overcome. Here are some suggestions for resisting peer pressure:.

- With friends and peers who might be pressuring you to view porn, it's important to establish boundaries.

Express your desire to avoid engaging in actions that might jeopardize your recovery and your efforts to overcome your addiction.

- Seek support: Surround yourself with friends and peers who are supportive of your efforts to overcome your addiction and who won't put any pressure on you to take part in actions that are detrimental to your recovery.

- Find healthy activities to partake in: Pursue healthy pastimes and interests that can replace watching porn. With a sense of purpose and accomplishment, this can lessen the chance of relapsing.

- Consider getting professional assistance from a mental health professional, like a therapist or counselor, who can offer direction and support in your attempts to beat your addiction.

- Practice self-care: Look after your physical and emotional needs by getting enough sleep, maintaining a healthy diet, and taking part in activities that help you unwind and cope with stress.

In order to resist peer pressure and kick a porn habit, it is crucial to establish boundaries, look for support, partake in healthy activities, get professional assistance, and practice self-care.

HOW TO HANDLE RELATIONSHIP ISSUES TO AVOID PORN

Relationship problems are frequently the cause of pornographic use because it provides a short-term escape from difficult emotions and conflicts. You can use the following techniques to deal with relationship problems and lessen your likelihood of turning to pornography:

- Discuss your feelings and concerns with your partner while also considering their perspective. When communicating, refrain from criticizing or blaming others and make an effort to be open and truthful.

- Seek professional help: You might want to consider speaking with a therapist or counselor if you're having difficulty expressing yourself clearly or resolving conflicts in your relationship. A mental health professional can provide guidance and encouragement as you work through your challenges.

- Make time for yourself and prioritize your own health by taking care of yourself. Spend time engaging in activities that bring you joy and relaxation, and take breaks as needed.

- Practice forgiving others: Forgiving others is a difficult but necessary task that is frequently required for relationship repair and healing. Consider expressing your regret to your partner and making an effort to forgive them.

- Describe your relationship issues to friends and family and solicit their suggestions. Ask your family and friends for help.

Remembering that overcoming a porn addiction is a process and that developing healthy coping skills may take some time and effort is crucial. Always remember to treat yourself nicely and to ask for help when you require it.

General Steps to take to beat Pornography Addiction

- Seek professional assistance: Take into consideration discussing your porn addiction with a mental health professional, such as a therapist or counselor. They can assist you in discovering the underlying causes of your addiction and creating coping mechanisms to deal with it.

- Determine triggers: Try to determine what makes you want to watch porn. It might be a particular feeling, an occasion, or a particular hour of the day. As soon as you identify the factors that make you want to watch porn, you can devise plans to prevent or manage those factors.

- Find healthy coping strategies: Rather than turning to pornography to deal with stress or unpleasant emotions, look for healthy coping strategies. Exercise, time with friends and family, and engaging in a hobby you enjoy are a few options.

- Find a partner for accountability: If you need support in your efforts to kick your addiction, think about finding a trusted friend or relative. You might also think about signing up for a support system like a 12-step program or a recovery group.

- Take good care of your physical well-being by ensuring that you get enough sleep, eat a balanced diet, and exercise frequently. It may be simpler to kick an addiction if you take care of your physical health because doing so can also help with your mental health and general wellbeing.

Be patient with yourself because getting over an addiction takes time and effort. Ask for help when you need it from friends, family, and professionals, and don't be embarrassed to do so.

CHAPTER FOUR: UNDERSTANDING PORN TRIGGERS AND OTHER KEY TERMS

WHAT ARE PORN TRIGGERS?

Anything that can make someone feel the urge to partake in a particular behavior, like watching pornography, is a trigger. Triggers can be internal (like a particular emotion or thought) or external (like a circumstance or environment). The following are some typical porn addiction triggers.

Anxiety or stress are common causes of people to turn to porn.

Boredom: When bored or without anything else to do, some people may watch porn.

Loneliness: Watching porn may momentarily make you feel less alone or isolated.

Porn can be used by some people as a coping mechanism for negative emotions like anger or frustration.

Curiosity: Out of a desire for novelty or excitement, some people may become interested in pornography and begin viewing it.

Relationship issues: When a person is having trouble in a romantic relationship, they may turn to porn as a coping mechanism or a means of escaping their problems.

Knowing your own unique triggers will help you create management or avoidance plans for them.

What Exactly Is The 12-step Program?

The 12-step program is a collection of tenets outlining a strategy for overcoming addiction, compulsive behaviors, or other behavioral issues. The 12 steps were created by Alcoholics Anonymous (AA) as a method of alcoholism recovery, but many other organizations, such as Narcotics Anonymous (NA) and Sex Addicts Anonymous (SAA), have adopted them and use them today.

The following are typically included in the 12 steps:.

1. Admitting that one's addiction is out of control and that their life has gotten out of control.

2. Believing that one can return to sanity by surrendering to a power greater than oneself.

3. Choosing to entrust this higher power with your will and your life.

4. Assessing one's moral character in a thorough and fearless manner.

5. Expressing the precise nature of one's wrongs to a higher power, oneself, and another person.

6. Being completely willing to allow a higher power to purge all of these character flaws.

7. Humbly pleading with a higher power to purge these character flaws.

8. Making a list of all the people one has hurt and deciding to make amends to them all.

9. Wherever possible, make amends to these people, unless doing so would harm them or others.

10. Keeping a running list of one's own accomplishments and owning up to mistakes.

11. Praying only for knowledge of a higher power's will for you and the ability to carry it out, while also attempting to improve your conscious connection with them through meditation and prayer.

12. Having experienced a spiritual awakening as a result of these actions, spreading this message to those who are suffering, and applying these guidelines to all of one's dealings.

The 12-step program is meant to be a spiritual program, and a person's personal religious beliefs can have a significant impact on how they interpret the idea of a "higher power.". Others may interpret this as a higher principle or the combined power of a group, while some may see this as God or another superior being. The development of a new way of life and personal transformation are the program's main goals.

FINDING ACCOUNTABILITY

Being held responsible for your actions while also receiving support and encouragement can be a useful tool in the fight against addiction. For finding accountability, consider these suggestions:.

- Find a dependable friend or family member: Take into account contacting a friend or relative you can trust to help you on your path to recovery from addiction. This person can act as your accountability partner and assist in keeping you responsible for your actions.

- Join a support group: You can connect with people who are battling addiction by joining a support group, such as a 12-step program or a recovery group. A sense of accountability and community can be fostered by these organizations.

- Consider seeking professional assistance: To discuss your addiction, think about meeting with a therapist or counselor who specializes in mental health. They can help you develop coping mechanisms for your addiction and offer support and direction.

- Take advantage of technology: There are many apps and websites that can assist you in tracking your progress and maintaining accountability. You could, for instance, use an app to monitor your screen time or to restrict access to particular websites.

Keep in mind that accountability is only one piece of the solution and works best when combined with other tactics like getting professional assistance, avoiding triggers, and developing healthy coping mechanisms.

USEFUL SOFTWARE IN COMBATING PORN ADDICTION

You can take control of your online habits and manage your addiction to porn through a number of software programs. The following is a list of some possibilities:

Freedom: This app allows you to block websites and apps on your phone and computer, setting limits on your screen time and helping you to stay focused on your goals.

StayFocusd: This Chrome extension helps you manage your time on the internet by blocking distracting websites and allowing you to set limits on your daily usage.

Cold Turkey: This app allows you to block specific websites or the entire internet for a set amount of time, helping you to stay focused and avoid distractions.

SelfControl: This app allows you to block access to distracting websites and emails for a set amount of time, helping you to stay on track and avoid temptation.

Covenant Eyes: This app and website monitoring service allows you to track your online activity and receive accountability reports, helping you to stay accountable and develop healthy online habits.

K9 Web Protection: This internet filter and website blocking software allows you to block inappropriate content and set limits on your online activity.

Net Nanny: This internet filtering and parental control software allows you to block inappropriate websites and set limits on your online activity.

Qustodio: This internet filtering and parental control software allows you to monitor your online activity and set limits on your screen time, helping you to develop healthy online habits.

PornAway: This Android app blocks porn websites and helps to protect you from inappropriate content.

LeechBlock: This browser extension allows you to block specific websites or categories of websites, helping you to stay focused and avoid distractions.

Freedom: https://freedom.to
StayFocusd:
https://chrome.google.com/webstore/detail/stayfo
cusd/laankejkbhbdhmipfmgcngdelahlfoji
Cold Turkey: https://getcoldturkey.com
SelfControl: https://selfcontrolapp.com
Covenant Eyes: https://www.covenanteyes.com
K9 Web Protection:
https://www1.k9webprotection.com
Net Nanny: https://www.netnanny.com
Qustodio: https://www.qustodio.com
PornAway: https://f-
droid.org/en/packages/com.github.pornaway/
LeechBlock: https://addons.mozilla.org/en-
US/firefox/addon/leechblock/

Here is a breakdown of the cost for each of the software programs I mentioned:

Freedom: The basic version of Freedom is free, but there is also a paid version with additional features.
StayFocusd: This Chrome extension is free.

Cold Turkey: The basic version of Cold Turkey is free, but there is also a paid version with additional features.

SelfControl: This app is free.

Covenant Eyes: This app and website monitoring service has a free trial, but a subscription is required for ongoing use.

K9 Web Protection: The basic version of K9 Web Protection is free, but there is also a paid version with additional features.

Net Nanny: This internet filtering and parental control software has a free trial, but a subscription is required for ongoing use.

Qustodio: This internet filtering and parental control software has a free trial, but a subscription is required for ongoing use.

PornAway: This Android app is free.

LeechBlock: This browser extension is free.

CHAPTER FIVE: SEEKING PROFESSIONAL ASSISTANCE

A crucial first step in beating a porn addiction is to seek professional assistance. I know this can be challenging for some people, thus I've dedicated an entire chapter to this topic.

WHY SHOULD YOU SEEK PROFESSIONAL HELP?

- A mental health expert, such as a therapist or counselor, can assist you in understanding the underlying factors that may be causing your addiction, such as past trauma, stress, or relationship issues. With professional assistance, you can gain a deeper understanding of the causes of your addiction. This can be useful when creating a strategy to deal with and get rid of your addiction.

- A mental health professional can offer you specific techniques and strategies for managing your addiction, such as cognitive-behavioral therapy, which can assist you in altering unhelpful thought patterns and behaviors.

- Working with a mental health professional can offer support and encouragement as you strive to overcome your addiction. When you run into difficulties, they can offer advice and motivation.

- Any underlying mental health problems can be addressed with professional assistance. Porn addiction can occasionally be a sign of a mental health problem, such as depression or anxiety. Your overall mental health can be improved by working with a mental health professional to address any underlying problems.

In general, getting professional assistance can be a crucial first step in beating a porn addiction and regaining control over your life.

THERAPY AND TREATMENT OPTIONS TYPES

The recovery from a porn addiction can be aided by a variety of therapies and treatments. A few choices are as follows:.

- Cognitive-behavioral therapy (CBT): This form of treatment enables patients to recognize and alter unhelpful thought processes and behaviors. By assisting people in coming up with ways to withstand the urge to watch pornography and in altering the underlying beliefs and behaviors that fuel the addiction, CBT can be helpful in managing a porn addiction.

- DBT, or dialectical behavior therapy, is a form of therapy that can be effective in reducing impulsivity and fostering positive coping skills. Due to its ability to help people recognize and alter unhealthy or unhelpful behaviors, it can be especially helpful in recovering from a porn addiction.

- Group therapy: Because it fosters a sense of belonging and support, group therapy can help people who are trying to kick a porn habit. Additionally, group therapy can offer a secure setting for discussing difficulties and exchanging coping mechanisms with others who are going through a similar ordeal.

- Family therapy: Dealing with interpersonal problems that might be causing a porn addiction can be a benefit of family therapy. Additionally, it can serve as a forum for relatives to talk about the effects of the addiction and to come up with plans for helping the person in their recovery.

- Medication: In some circumstances, therapy and medication may be combined to help manage a porn addiction. A porn addiction, for instance, can be exacerbated by underlying mental health issues like depression or anxiety, which some people may benefit from taking medication for.

Working with a mental health professional will help you choose the most appropriate course of action for your unique needs and circumstances.

THERAPIST VERSUS TREATMENT CENTER.

When seeking treatment for a porn addiction, there are some differences between visiting a therapist and going to a facility. Here are a few notable variations:

- Setting: While a treatment center is a residential facility where people live while receiving treatment, a therapist typically sees clients in an office setting.

- Treatment duration: Therapy sessions can last for an indefinite amount of time and are typically ongoing. A set program lasting for a set amount of time, such as 30 days or 90 days, may be part of the treatment at a treatment facility, which is typically more intensive.

- Structure: Treatment at a treatment facility is typically more regimented and adheres to a set schedule; therapy sessions with a therapist may be more adaptable and involve less structure.

- Services offered: Treatment facilities frequently provide a wider range of services, including individual therapy, group therapy, and recreational activities, whereas private therapy may concentrate more on one-on-one sessions.

- Cost: Therapy sessions with an outpatient therapist may be less expensive than those at treatment facilities. When deciding which option is best for you, it's critical to take your budget and insurance coverage into account.

- Level of commitment: Attending a treatment facility necessitates a sizeable time commitment and might entail taking time away from work or other obligations. For those who have other commitments, seeing a therapist on an outpatient basis might be a more convenient option.

- Addiction severity: A treatment facility may offer the best option for those who have a severe addiction because it offers a higher level of intensive care. Outpatient therapy sessions with a therapist might be sufficient for those with less severe addictions.

- Personal preference: Your needs and preferences will ultimately determine which choice is best for you. It might be beneficial to think about your comfort level and what you believe will help you overcome your addiction the most.

WHAT TO LOOK OUT FOR IN CHOOSING A THERAPIST

There are a few things you should look out for to make sure you find a qualified and successful therapist when looking for one to help you overcome a porn addiction:.

- Make sure the therapist you are considering has the required training and credentials, such as a license to practice therapy, by checking their training and credentials. This will guarantee that they are certified to offer therapy services.

- Experience: Think about hiring a therapist who has handled cases of porn addicts in the past. They'll be more cognizant of the particular problems and difficulties you might be dealing with.

- Specialization: Some psychotherapists may focus on treating issues like porn addiction or other specialized problems. Think about seeing a counselor who specializes in these topics.

- Consider a therapist whose method is in line with your values and objectives. For instance, if you favor a more holistic approach, you might want to think about working with a therapist who uses complementary therapies like mindfulness.

- Finding a therapist with whom you are comfortable and who you can trust is crucial. Think about whether you click with the therapist and whether you think they're a good fit for you.

Just keep in mind that it might take some time and a few tries to find the right therapist for you. Until you find a therapist who feels like a good fit, don't be afraid to shop around and try out various practitioners.

WHAT TO LOOK OUT FOR IN CHOOSING A TREATMENT CENTER

There are a few things to keep an eye out for when looking for a treatment facility to help you overcome a porn addiction to make sure you find a qualified and efficient facility:.

- Make sure the treatment facility you are thinking about has accreditation from a reputable agency, like the Joint Commission. This will guarantee that they adhere to strict safety and quality standards.

- Check the treatment facility's license to see if it is authorized to offer therapy in your state.

- Staff qualifications: Take into account the education, experience, and training of the treatment center's staff. Make sure they have the training necessary to give you the care you require.

- Service offerings: Take into account the treatment facility's service offerings, which include recreational activities, group therapy, and individual therapy. Make sure the treatment facility provides the services you require to achieve your treatment objectives.

- Aftercare: Take a look at the aftercare services that the rehab facility provides, such as assistance with reintegrating into society and maintaining recovery after treatment.

- Cost: Take into account the treatment center's fee schedule and whether it fits into your spending plan. Be sure to confirm what is covered with your insurance company.

- Location: Think about where the treatment facility is located and whether it is easy for you to get to.

Do your research and take your time to find a treatment facility that suits your unique needs and circumstances.

CHAPTER SIX: THE WAY FORWARD

DIFFERENCE BETWEEN A LAPSE AND A RELAPSE

A lapse is a brief setback or slip in the process of recovering from addiction, whereas a relapse is the return of addictive behavior after a period of recovery.

A lapse can happen when a person has a craving for their drug of choice or exhibits a behavior linked to their addiction but does not go back to abusing it fully. A lapse does not necessarily indicate that a person has fully relapsed; it can be a common occurrence during the healing process.

A relapse, on the other hand, is a period of recovery followed by a return to full-blown addictive behavior. It might entail completely restarting use of the drug of choice or regularly engaging in the addictive behavior. Relapse can be a major obstacle to recovery and may call for additional care or assistance.

To stop a lapse from developing into a full-blown relapse, it's crucial to understand the difference between a lapse and a relapse and to seek support when necessary.

PREVENTING A RELAPSE INTO PORN

Here are a few methods to use in order to avoid relapsing while in recovery from a porn addiction:

- Making a list of the circumstances, ideas, and emotions that make you want to watch pornographic material will help you identify your triggers. This can assist you in developing a plan to avoid your triggers and increasing your awareness of them.

- Create healthy coping mechanisms that you can use to control your triggers and cravings by working with a therapist or counselor to develop your coping skills. Spending time with friends and family, exercising, or engaging in meditation are a few examples of what this could entail.

- Ask for help: As you attempt to avoid a relapse, it is crucial to ask for help from friends, family, and professionals. This may entail attending therapy or counseling as well as joining a support group, such as a 12-step program or a recovery group.

- Make use of technology: Think about using apps or software to help you keep track of your online habits. Apps that monitor your screen time or restrict access to particular websites may fall under this category.

- Establish accountability: Think about finding an accountability partner, such as a dependable friend or relative, or enrolling in a support group or 12-step program where you can be held accountable for your deeds.

- Practice self-care: To aid in your recovery and ward off relapse, engage in regular self-care activities like exercise, sleep, and a healthy diet.

Keep in mind that preventing a relapse is a continuous process that calls for ongoing work and dedication. It's crucial to take charge of your recovery and to ask for help when you need it.

ADDITIONAL STEPS

Now that you are on the right track towards according your goal of overcome porn addiction, here are a few additional steps you can take to continue on your road to recovery after overcoming a porn addiction:

- Celebrate your success: Take some time to acknowledge your accomplishments and the effort you put forth to beat your addiction.

- Keep up your self-care routines to support your recovery and keep making progress, such as regular exercise, rest, and healthy eating.

- Seek on-going support: To maintain your recovery and connect with others who are going through similar difficulties, think about joining a support group or continuing therapy.

- Take some time to consider your journey and the advancements you have made. You may find it easier to maintain your motivation and concentration by doing this.

- Create new objectives: Think about creating new objectives for your personal, professional, or spiritual lives. This can aid in your ongoing personal growth and development.

Keep in mind that recovery is a lifelong process that calls for ongoing effort and commitment. To maintain your recovery, it's critical to be on guard and to ask for help when you need it.

AUTHOR'S AFTERWORD

Here are some words of advice and encouragement from my personal experience for people who are trying to kick a porn habit:.

Remember that you are not alone in your struggles and that many other people have been able to successfully recover from a porn addiction.

The possibility of change exists, despite the fact that it can occasionally be challenging. You can beat your addiction and create a fulfilling life if you put in the necessary time and effort.

Don't be afraid to ask friends, family, and professionals for support. There are numerous resources available to assist you in kicking your addiction.

Be patient with yourself because it takes time and effort to overcome an addiction. It's critical to be kind to yourself and to acknowledge your accomplishments as you go.

Continue: Don't let failures or lapses deter you. Keep going and never forget that you have what it takes to beat your addiction.

Keep in mind that you can conquer your addiction and create a fulfilling, healthy life. You can take charge of your recovery and accomplish your objectives with effort and resolve.

For those who have already conquered their addictions:

Being able to overcome an addiction is a significant accomplishment and something you should be proud of. Spend some time acknowledging your accomplishments and the effort you put into your recovery.

You are able to overcome any challenge: By successfully kicking your addiction, you have already shown that you are strong and determined. Keep in mind that you are capable of overcoming any challenge you may encounter.

Do not let your addiction define you; keep moving forward. Keep going and concentrate on leading a healthy, fulfilling life.

Seek on-going assistance: To keep up your recovery and connect with others dealing with comparable issues, think about joining a support group or continuing your therapy.

Believe in yourself: Have faith in your capacity to design a happy, fulfilling life. You have the capacity to fulfill your potential and accomplish your objectives.

Always keep in mind that recovery is a lifelong journey that calls for continued effort and dedication. To maintain your recovery, it's crucial to be watchful and to ask for help when you need it.

Conclusion

I recognize how difficult it can be to kick a porn habit. It can be a challenging and overwhelming process, but I want you to know that you can beat your addiction and regain control of your life. I can attest from personal experience that pornography can be addictive and have a negative impact on interpersonal relationships, employment prospects, and general wellbeing. However, I am aware that change is conceivable. It requires time and work, so it's important to be patient with yourself and ask for help when you need it. Don't be reluctant to ask friends, family, and experts for assistance. Keep in mind that you are not alone in your struggle and that others have beaten a porn addiction. You can take charge of your recovery and accomplish your goals if you put in the necessary effort.